Getting

Scrapbooking

How to Create Your First Scrapbook

By Phyllis Matthews

Disclaimer

ISBN-13: 978-1500328795
ISBN-10: 1500328790

Table of Contents

CHAPTER I. MAKING YOUR FIRST SCRAPBOOK. HOW TO BEGIN

You have memories you want to preserve. You have seen some beautiful, even inspiring scrapbooks that are urging you to try your hand at this craft, but perhaps you feel overwhelmed at the prospect. Well cast your fears aside!

Everything you'll need to get started is right here in this book. Don't like lessons? Too much like school? Well read on while I let you in on my secrets. The first one is that making a scrapbook is really fun!

Scrapbooking combines the best parts of many other crafts, some of which may have already tried. You get to choose colors and styles just like with designing a line of clothing. You get to measure and cut just like sewing an outfit. You get to paste and join smaller objects together like a master carpenter building a fine piece of furniture. You get to layer elements of design much like an interior decorator. With scrapbooking you get to bring it all together for something beautiful that you, your friends and family can enjoy for many years to come!

The secret is that all crafts involve the same basic skills and they all evolve from a basic core of creativity. If you can do any of them, more than likely you could do them all.

Perhaps you don't know where to start, or what to buy. Are you afraid to invest in a lot of tools and supplies because you're unsure if you will want to continue? Start for free and gradually work your way up. Free? Yes! Your thoughts are free, and your ideas only cost as much as a notebook or some scratch paper to begin your plans. Here is the typical beginning of a scrapbook and the way I always start any projects.

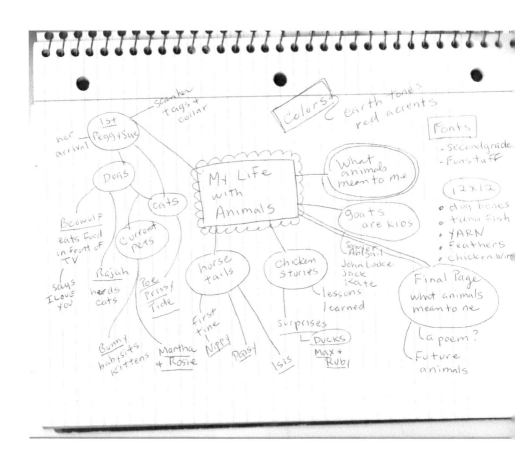

This is the actual mind map that was the beginning of a digital scrapbook I created. That is another option you might want to consider. It is a different medium altogether, and many scrapbookers prefer this method. A later chapter deals with many of the issues involved with this popular new trend.

All you need is a piece of blank paper and a pencil. That's right, not a pen, because you will want to erase as you go along. Don't worry if it looks messy. Creative minds are not neat—they are very messy. If you're more computer savvy, there are mind-map programs available that you may find more to your liking. Either method works fine, so do whatever works best for you. I'm old-school and find a piece of paper and pencil work best for me.

The purpose of this exercise is to map out what's in your mind. It is to get you started and to inspire you. It should not be cast in stone—or even permanent ink. Just jot it down into a notebook, or a scrap of paper (how appropriate for a scrapbook beginning), or just scribble something on the back of an old envelope or piece of junk mail. You can throw it away later. And you don't even need to stick to it if inspiration leads you in another direction.

Those of you who are computer geeks might prefer creating something in a drawing program. That way you can edit it until you're happy with it. Just throw your ideas out there freely until it represents what you want to accomplish in your scrapbook. Like all things, this gets easier the more you do it.

It may seem like a simple idea, but it works. This bare-bones map helps make it real in your mind. It's a starting point. Just doodle. Your brain does amazing things all on its own when you let it play with an idea.

This is the scrapbook that resulted from my idea map. Yes, that is a goat on the bed. And yes, that is a chicken sitting with a new brood of baby ducks. Enough about my scrapbook. Now let's talk about *your* scrapbook, the one that's still in your head.

CHAPTER II. YOUR PICTURES—THE TRUE BEGINNING OF EVERY SCRAPBOOK

The pages of a scrapbook are built around the pictures. In the era of digital photography everyone has hundreds of pictures. All you need to do is choose the most special ones and decide what sizes you want the prints to be.

Usually, the pictures you want are scattered among mixed media. Some on your hard drive and not labeled in any retrievable fashion. Some are in your camera among hundreds of others and you can't even remember what's in there. Some are in albums, cardboard boxes, and file folders (the actual manila type). Some are on CD's, flash drives or even some type of archaic floppy disk. Some need to be scanned. And some may be in the possession of other people, like the time you forgot your camera and your sister took all the pictures at the event. Yes, it happens.

Well, here's a tip for organizing pictures for a scrapbook. Make a folder on your desktop and call it *"name* scrapbook." Then gather and examine all your pictures, make your decisions and copy them into this folder. Rename the pictures according to the subject and number them. This will allow you to keep track of how many pages to plan for.

Yes, you really should compile all your photos into one place, organize them, label them, and then make a proper backup. Do that some other time or you will never get around to making your first scrapbook.

I am not a photographer, but perhaps you are. No wonder you are drawn to scrapbooking. But most people who make scrapbooks are not, yet they manage to make wonderful works of art. Here is the next secret: Editing, Cropping (with or without scissors), and Improvising.

Almost every photo printing service offers a number of basic editing features. You can greatly improve a picture by simply lightening or darkening it. Sometimes cropping out the undesirable background or zooming in to a subject changes the entire feel of a photo.

There are even programs that allow you to convert an ordinary photograph into an oil painting or drawing in pastels, chalk, or charcoal. Here's a hint- if you spend a lot of time and energy on a particular photo, place it largely on a page as a single feature and highly embellish it to draw a lot of attention to your work of art.

Here are some basic things you can do with simple editing. You need to be careful not to blow up a small part of a picture too large or you will lose quality. Also, be sure to save your original under a different name just in case you change your mind or need it for another project.

I cropped this to a portrait orientation without losing any quality.

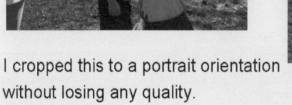

Cropping with scissors is sometimes the better option. Print your pictures in whatever size you like, but usually the 4 x 6 option is the easiest to work with. One reason for cutting down your pictures is that you need to fit a whole lot of them on your page. If you crop them through photo editing you will end up with the same size as the original, less quality, and no solution to your problem. It's easier to show this than explain it.

Using a photo editing appication results in a slight loss in quality.

Original photo cropped with scissors. No loss in resolution, plus it fits better on the page.

Another advantage to cropping the pictures after printing is that you can use decorative scissors to get a fancy edge. Don't worry if you don't have those yet. The idea of spending a lot of money on supplies before you've even made your first scrapbook might make you want to forget the whole thing. You can get a decorative edge simply by adding an attractive trim or decorative paper behind your photo.

If you don't have decorative edge scissors, crop your photo then cut out a background from a piece of scrap paper. Same affect.

Improvising is what you need to do if you absolutely cannot find or adapt a picture for the event or subject in your scrapbook. It happens. You forget your camera or your batteries die on you. Use ticket stubs, program flyers, newspaper clippings, train or bus schedules, decorations, postcards, invitations, receipts, brochures, maps or just your own words to create a spectacular page. Also add stickers or some clip art from your computer.

This happened to me on a trip to New Orleans. It was a long time ago, and it was when I was just a beginner at scrapbooking—like you. You know what? That scrapbook means the world to me, and I enjoy looking through it just as much as my later fancier ones. In fact, I have considered making it over using all the techniques I've learned since then, but I just can't bring myself to do it. It had become special because of its primitive look. Don't be intimidated by the scrapbooks you've seen—just get busy and make one!

This book was done entirely without photos. You don't believe me? You think you see pictures. It looks like photos of a balcony and a mule wearing a hat, doesn't it? Those are postcards. I also cut out graphics from brochures and maps. Add personal notes and stories abundantly to make up for the fact that you won't be in there. Use maps and circle where you were or make comments about the things you saw and did.

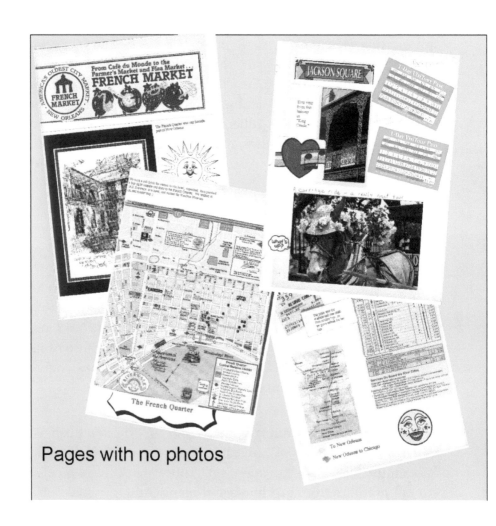

Pages with no photos

My daughter was recently looking at this scrapbook, and it was quite moving for her to remember that trip. She was so young back then. It did distress her to see the yellowing already beginning to deteriorate the pages. As I said, this was from before I knew the correct methods. Don't let that happen to you. **Remember: Acid-free is the key.**

So enough about that. Let's move on to finishing your first scrapbook.

CHAPTER III. WHAT'S YOUR STYLE?

It's not so much a matter of deciding on a format, it's all about knowing your personal style. Your scrapbook should reflect *you*—unless it's a gift for someone else. In that case concentrate on the other person's style.

Your scrapbook should be composed of things that you love. This may be easy. You may already know that you like whimsical or traditional or ultra-modern and cool. If not, look around you. What kinds of things do you surround yourself with? What are your favorite objects? Then ask yourself why. Is it the color? The meaning? The era it represents?

If that little exercise does not help, or if it only helps a little—go spend some time in your closet. No, not as punishment. Look at the clothing you have chosen to wear. This represents the image you want to show to the world. What colors do you choose? Into which category would you place your wardrobe? Is it cute? Sultry and sexy? Feminine or old-fashioned? Country? Corporate executive? Sensible? Or absolutely far out crazy?

The kind of cover you choose, as well as the designed pages inside, should be something that makes you smile when you look at it. The only reason I ever buy an album with a completely blank cover is so that I can embellish it to my heart's desire. When you reach the point where you have an entire trunk full of scrapbooks, you will appreciate that each one has a distinctive cover. You will not be able to find a particular one among your collection if the covers are a simple solid color.

This is just a small sample of the variety of albums you can create. Go to a craft store or look online just to see what's out there before you decide on your first. It doesn't mean you have to buy it there. Go to discount stores, thrift shops, and yard sales. I hardly ever pass up a bargain scrapbook when I find one at a good price—even if I don't like the color. That can be changed. I've re-covered albums with cloth, glued on embellishments, and even painted them. Notice the kitten album in the example? I changed it to a Christmas book by adding holiday stickers, charms, and trims so that it would appear as if the cats were playing with ornaments.

The Arkansas scrapbook already had a window cut-out design on the cover to reveal the first page. I created a vellum pocket instead and filled it with confetti. The book I made to commemorate the birth of my twin granddaughters ended up bulging way too much so I used a drapery tie-back in matching colors to help hold it shut. I used metallic mailbox numbers from the hardware store to make my 2012 book. Once you become a full-fledged scrapbooking addict (like me) you will see things you can use for your craft everywhere you go.

CHAPTER IV. PAGE DESIGN—THE NITTY GRITTY OF SCRAPBOOKING

Your pictures are going to determine much of your page layout. Here are the steps to making it work. Sort them. It may seem a simple step, but it will make the whole project easier.

After you have your package of printed pictures, divide them up according to the pages on which they will appear. You will not get the entire scrapbook finished in a day. Consider yourself lucky if you get a page or two done at each session. So you need to have a plan—not that you can't change your mind a little as you proceed. Remember to think in terms of a double-page spread, except for the title page and the final page which are singles.

Use envelopes, folders, or cardboard dividers to separate your pictures according to subject or event. If you don't do this, guess what can happen? You end up finishing an entire page only later to find a stray picture that belongs there after it's too late. Grrrr!

You may have as many as 30 photos or more for an occasion such as a birthday party. In that case, you may want to divide the pages into such categories as "opening presents", "blowing out candles", "eating cake", "games", etc. In a scrapbook that covers an entire year, you will want to pare down the pictures so that a party is represented by a single double-page spread. Or, if you are devoting an entire book to an event, such as a graduation or a wedding, you will divide the event into multiple pages with fewer pictures on each page.

Make a plan like this. The numerals refer to the number of pictures you have to place on each page. Insert whatever quantity of double-pages you need to complete your book within the front and back pages—which are single pages. This will help you to plan the layout for your pages as well as estimate the amount of supplies you will need to decorate them.

Use the space alongside your page diagram to make notes about features you want to include in that layout, color schemes, embellishments you want to use, etc.

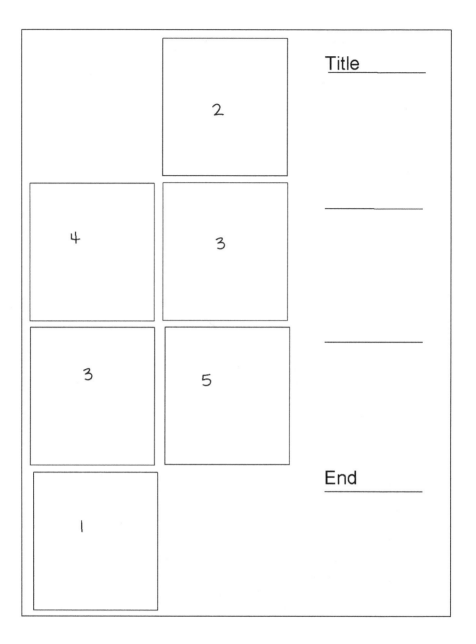

This is just an example. It only shows six pages. In actuality, there will be more like twenty for a typical scrapbook. You could make your own style diagram on notebook paper or in a computer application. Use any kind of program that allows you to draw rectangle shapes or create something like a table in two columns plus a third for your notes.

Once you have your general plan in mind, you are to the point of beginning your first page. You need to decide on your page designs. Lay out your paper which is the same size as the pages in your book and *lay* them *out*. First do this to see *if* they fit, then decide *how* they will fit. You will be using cropped photos for this part of the process. Crop them using scissors, a paper cutter, or even an X-Acto knife.

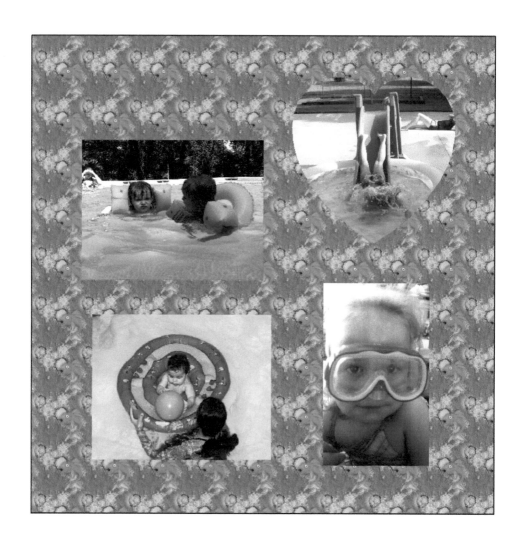

At this point the pictures are just sitting on top of the paper. You are playing with the idea of a layout design. Decide on a background that compliments your pictures and conveys your image. Notice how I chose the orange fish because of the orange ball in the photo? At this point I considered using orange matting for the photos a well.

Now is the time to consider the colors you might want to use for matting your pictures, where you might want to place the title for this spread, and how much room you will need for journaling. That could be a few words, a sentence, or a full page story depending on what it will take to explain what is happening.

Just Like Fish

Joy graduated away from floaties, and the twins were pretty jealous. The adults were just happy to keep cool.

This is what the page would look like with the picture cropped, the matting applied, the page title inserted and the journaling box created. Create all your elements off the page and permanently attach them only after you are sure they are what you want. That way, if you make a mistake, you only need to remake a single small portion of the page and not ruin everything.

At this stage, choose background design, title styles, matting colors, decorations, and journaling space. The best way to go is to make your choices based on the colors and subject matter of the pictures themselves. If your background is busy, it is even more important that you set the photos apart and make them pop. Keep this in mind regarding the title and the journaling spaces.

If you want to cut out cute shapes, use cookie cutters. But unless you have clear acrylic ones or hollow ones, be careful not to chop off parts of your picture you wanted to keep.

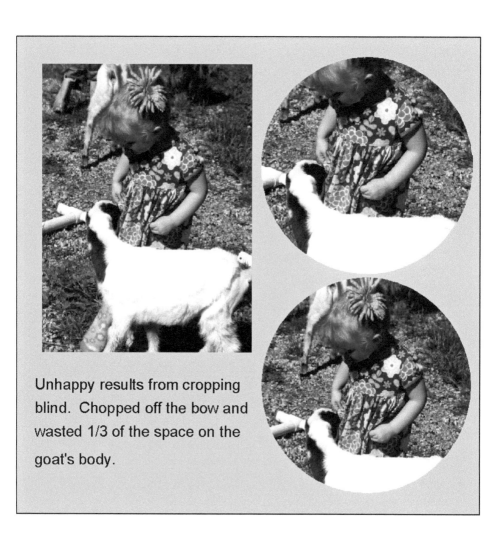

Unhappy results from cropping
blind. Chopped off the bow and
wasted 1/3 of the space on the
goat's body.

You might notice a rather undesirable feature right above the child's head. Cropping it out is a consideration, but that would also eliminate the cute bow. There is another solution. Add an embellishment on the page to cover only the part you want to eliminate. A sticker would work great. Just overlap a cute farm animal graphic so that at least a tiny part of it covers any inappropriate parts of your photos.

Here is a method to help prevent such mistakes. Don't just draw around your cookie cutter with a pen on your photo. This is a bad idea, not only because you may be cropping incorrectly, but because most ink is acidic and will eventually destroy the chemicals in your photo and ruin it.

The best way is to first draw your shape onto a piece of tracing paper then place the paper over your picture until it is in the correct position. Tape it in place on a section that is going to become scrap, then draw over the outline with a sharp pen or pencil. The impression should be visible enough for you to make your cut. This won't work if you choose too intricate a design.

Here is an ideal crop. The cute bow is showing, her hands are exposed enough to see what she is doing, and there is enough of the goat to see what it is and yet not waste space on its body.

What if you are not a baker and you don't have a bunch of cute cookie cutters in your kitchen drawer? You can buy stencils. The simplest shapes will work best for you as a beginner. Try the kids' craft department. The ones at the hobby stores can be quite elaborate, therefore a little intimidating, and will also cost a lot more money. After you've done one or two scrapbooks (and realize you're hooked) then feel free to add to your collection as much as your budget will allow.

Here are some samples of layouts to get you started.

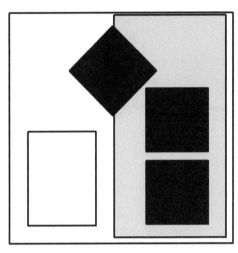

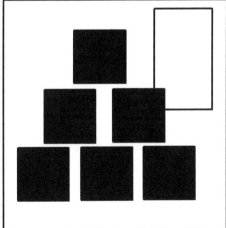

The sky is the limit. You can find lots of sample layout designs for free online. It's not stealing. Well, most of the time it isn't. Look for scrapbooking websites created by enthusiasts who simply want to share ideas. There are scrapbooking Facebook pages and you can find lots on Pinterest or Etsy.

CHAPTER V. PUTTING IT ALL TOGETHER

The final step in creating a scrapbook is adding the embellishments. Here is where you can get carried away and spend some serious money. Don't worry. You don't have to do it all at once. I'm on a budget myself, and I have found ways to make beautiful scrapbooks without all the expense. In fact some of my favorites are really simple, and you might want to start this way.

Here is a page I made with a scrap of patterned computer paper, some crinkled tissue, a sprig of artificial flowers, and a bit of yarn. A few eyelets from my sewing drawer, and I think the page is very complete. The torn paper effect is a cool technique. Tear toward you to create the white along the border. Depending on your color scheme, you could rub the raw edge with chalk.

If you already have experience with other crafts, you should include samples of that in your scrapbook. It will make it all the more personal and save money using materials you have on hand. I use a lot of sewing notions in my scrapbooks. If you draw or paint, try creating your own backgrounds. Then you won't need to spend money on expensive scrapbooking paper. They can easily cost a dollar per sheet or more—at least for the prettiest ones.

In this scrapbook, I created an unusual look made by brushing some water color around the edges. These are from a child's paint box that I borrowed from the toy box. As you can see, this required no talent whatsoever; you might call it child's play. I typed my journaling on a parchment paper and tore the edges. The photo is also printed on the same paper, and then I simply added some clip art.

Grandma didn't get to go on the Disney cruise—but the dresses she made for Hannah and Eden did.

42

If you are a sewer, add appliqués, lace trim, eyelets, rick-rack, or buttons to your pages. If you crochet or knit, yarn makes a wonderful decoration. It is also possible to sew through paper on your machine. You can do it without thread to make holes to attach crochet stitches. These buttons are sewn to ribbon, but you can attach buttons directly with a strong adhesive. Fake the stitches by inserting some tiny pieces of thread, ribbon, or even skinny strips of paper through the holes and glue the ends to the other side before attaching them to your page.

If you do decorative painting, decoupage, or rubber stamping—add those skills to your scrapbooking toolkit. You're half-way there before you even begin! In the sample page shown here, I actually glued cloth to the page which was leftover from the dresses featured in the pictures.

Another economical page was one in which I used a rubber stamp to create a background then journaled with a felt tipped-pen in a cute curvy pattern. On the opposite page I printed my message on common colored stock and attached it to matting made of natural fiber scraps. They call them scrapbooks for a reason.

The only consideration you will need to keep in mind it that your materials must be acid-free if they touch your photos. For a few dollars you can purchase an acid-testing pen. Consider this a worthwhile investment. You will need this if you are going to use materials that you haven't bought from a store. Everything sold for scrapbooking purposes will be labeled acid-free, including the glue.

This page uses chalk, stickers, stencils, and a picture from a greeting card. Here I did my journaling in my own handwritten words with a felt-tip pen (which was acid-free, of course).

This is something that causes many crafters to cringe in fear. So many of us do not like our own handwriting—even block printing, not to mention cursive.

Here's another one of my famous secrets—your handwriting will be very special to people as time passes. In later years, your loved ones will treasure the words you've penned on your pages. There is something very special about your own style of script. Over the years, I find myself pleased to find samples of my loved ones actual handwriting—whether in a letter, or on a document or a recipe—it carries a lot of sentiment.

If you still feel reluctant to write in your scrapbook, here are a few suggestions to make it easier. 1) Write on a separate paper first, and then attach it to your page so you won't worry about ruining your entire layout if you mess up. 2) Practice improving your handwriting using the lined paper you had in preschool. That's how you first learned, after all. Try re-training yourself. 3) Draw pencil lines on your journaling box. This will help you to keep your text straight and better judge the shape of your script.

CHAPTER VI. SETTING UP A PLACE TO WORK

For your first scrapbook, a kitchen table is a fine workspace—as long as you can keep other family members and pets away from it. This is not a hobby that you can complete in one session, nor is it one that you can tuck away easily into a drawer or satchel.

A desktop or table can work in a pinch.

If you start small, you can get by with one or two pairs of scissors, a few tubes of glue, some acid-free double sided tape, and a stack of paper. If you have followed my recommendations and are concentrating on one book which you have completely planned ahead, then you should only have a minimal amount of materials to deal with.

There are scrapbookers out there—so I'm told—who manage to keep all their supplies tucked away in a single crate or a suitcase. They take their portable workstation to events or from room to room as they work on their projects. Some plan for and buy materials for only one scrapbook at a time, limiting the amount of supplies they need to keep on hand. I have to admit I can't do that.

Something I used to use in the early days was a plastic bin with drawers on wheels. The widest ones come large enough to handle 12 x 12 papers. They can easily roll under a desk or table when not in use.

The thing I really like to recommend about this method is that it is expandable. You can buy more bins, stack them, and eventually make an entire wall into a scrapbooking area. You will eventually need a dedicated space in which to work—one with plenty of storage for you to organize your papers, stickers, pens, scissors, and other tools.

Start small with one plastic bin and then you can expand as your collection grows.

You will need a comfortable chair and good lighting. It doesn' t need to be fancy.

In no time, your first scrapbook will lead to another and another until you have to find space to keep them all as well as needing a dedicated area in which to work and store your materials. I have seen workstations set up inside old armoires or wardrobes. A space in a corner of the family room or a section of the basement will work.

But don't let any of that overwhelm you or keep you from starting that first scrapbook. Everything you need should fit into a single shopping bag you can tuck away into a closet until you finish it. Do all your planning first, then go shopping for the things you will need.

For your first project, keep your list short and sweet:

- ❖ Small, sharp scissors (and one or two decorative edge scissors if you want)

- ❖ An album

- ❖ Pictures

- ❖ Acid-free glue and double-sided tape

- ❖ Acid-free papers approximately one sheet for each page or improvise

- ❖ Acid-free felt-tip pens plus chalk, paint, etc. if desired

❖ Embellishments within reason—stickers, ribbons, buttons, etc.

If you are still reluctant to begin your first scrapbook you might want to experiment with digital scrapbooking to try your hand at it for free. Most of the sites that offer this product permit you to completely create, and even store, a complete scrapbook on their site (an online search for *Digital Scrapbooks* or *Digital Scrapbooking* will yield many such sites). You only pay when you actually order the book. Here you can practice your skills and get an idea if this is a craft you would enjoy. Many prefer this method exclusively. But not me. I prefer the textures and the three-dimensional aspects of actually dealing with paper, ribbon, glue, etc. This is, after all, what a real scrapbook is.

You will never know if you are one of those people unless you give it a try.

CHAPTER VII. FINAL WORDS

By now the question no longer is whether or not you want to make a scrapbook but which one to do first. Welcome to the crowd. You have lots of friends out there that you've never even met. Before this craze took over the country in the 1980's, people were making scrapbooks as far back as the mid-1800's.

Most of these lovingly created treasures did not survive the ages because there was no understanding about the acidity in paper. I have the remains of one my grandmother made around 1945, and it is still crumbling despite my efforts to preserve its contents. Whatever glue she used, it has hardened the pages into stiff sheets that can barely withstand even a gentle touch. I had to remove the pieces to keep the paper from doing even more damage as time goes on. These fragments are kept in a plastic box and wrapped with tissue paper, which is acid-free by the way.

Back in the old days—before photography had even been invented—people made scrapbooks using advertisements, notes, cards, clippings, and letters. My grandmother's book is unsophisticated and primitive. She even glued my baby food jar labels onto the page, probably having no idea how special it would be for me to see them in later years. Commercially prepared strained infant food was a relatively new phenomenon then. Whatever material they were made from disintegrated when I applied the glue solvent. She had cut out pictures from magazines that she liked, as well as obituaries and news stories that caught her interest. I have no idea why she saved receipts, but I do the same thing myself.

Mark Twain was a prolific scrapbooker, and he liked to carry his works-in-progress along with him on his travels. The inconvenience he experienced led him to create the first self-adhesive scrapbook which he patented in 1873. It was one of his few inventions that produced a moderate but reliable income. This is the advertising label from his product.

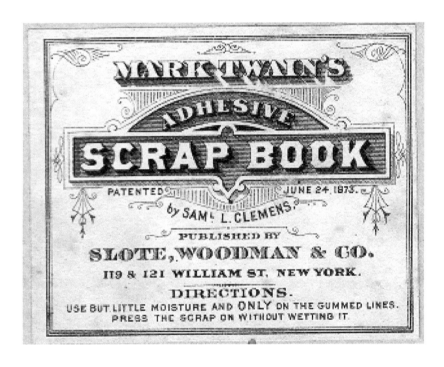

By now your dilemma is no longer how to get started on your first scrapbook, but which one you want to do first. The topics and styles from which to choose are limited only by your imagination. You will need a notebook to jot down your list of future plans for scrapbooks. Here is a partial list of ideas for scrapbooks to help you get started:

- An Annual Review, one of the most common types of scrapbooks

- A Book of goals, either for a lifetime or for the next year

- Things for which you're grateful; great for a Thanksgiving themed album

- A Day in My Life, perhaps as a mini-book

- The Women in my Life/Men in my Life; a tribute album to or for a loved one

- Growing Up _____ (fill the blank) Irish, German, Catholic, Jewish, In the Seventies, In the Good Old Days, With Crazy People, Broke, etc.

- An Affirmation Book filled with inspiring quotes, poems, or inspirations

- Your Life Story, or an ancestor's if you also do genealogy

- Before and After Book covering a weight loss story, make-over, or transition

- What I Like About_____ (fill the blank)

- A Bucket-List Book

- A Victory Book which tells the story of a miraculous recovery or overcoming an ordeal

The list is endless, but this book is not. It is time for you to put it aside now and begin your own adventure into the wonderful world of scrapbooking. Gather your materials, start your sketches, and make your lists! But most of all, don't forget to have fun. That's what this hobby is all about!

To your scrapbooking success!

OTHER BOOKS BY PHYLLIS MATTHEWS

If you enjoyed this book, then **Budget Scrapbooking for Beginners** will make a nice companion to this one. Here you will learn the secrets to many more creative ideas not found anywhere else! Learn how to make scrapbooks that are both beautiful and treasured, but don't break the bank in the process.

CPSIA information can be obtained
at www.ICGtesting.com
Printed in the USA
BVHW021004121221
623851BV00001B/4